My Name Is William Tell

My Name Is William Tell

Poems by
William Stafford

A James R. Hepworth Book

Confluence Press   ◄►   Lewiston, Idaho

Acknowledgements

Some of these poems originally appeared in the following magazines: *Alaska Fish and Game, Albatross, The American Poetry Review, The Amicus Journal, The American Scholar, The Atlantic, Audience, Blue Buildings, The Chariton Review, The Christian Science Monitor, The Chicago Tribune, Chrysalis, Concerning Poetry, Cottonwood, Crab Creek Review, Crazyhorse, Field, The Georgia Review, Hardscrabble, High Country News, High Rock Review, Inquiry, Jeopardy, L'Espirit, Lemming, The Memphis State Review, The Nation, Negative Capability, New Letters, The New Republic, The New York Quarterly, The New Yorker, Northwest Review, The Ohio Review, Oregon East, The Oregonian, The Pacific Review, Partisan Review, Perceptions, Pitt Poetry Series, Plainsong, The Poetry Miscellany, Poetry Now, Poetry Review, Poets On, Portland Review, Practices of the Wind, Preview, Prism, Quarterly West, Sandlapper, Scarab, The Southern Poetry Review, Stand, Tar River Poetry, Three Rivers, The Tower, Triquarterly, Tusitala, The Virginia Quarterly, Western Humanities Review, The Wittenberg Review, Yankee.*

Donnell Hunter selected and arranged the poems in this volume from six previous limited edition chapbooks that he printed on his letterpress in Rexburg, Idaho: *Stories and Storms and Strangers* (Honeybrook Press, 1984); *Brother Wind* (Honeybrook Press, 1986); *Annie-Over* (Honeybrook Press, 1988); *Fin, Feather, Fur* (Honeybrook Press, 1989); *How to Hold Your Arms When It Rains* (Confluence Press, 1990).

My Name Is William Tell received a 1992 Western States Book Award in poetry. The Western States Book Awards are a project of the Western States Arts Federation. The awards are supported by the Xerox Foundation, Crane Duplicating Service, and the Witter Bynner Foundation for Poetry. Additional Funding is provided by the National Endowment for the Arts Literature Program.

Publication of this book is made possible, in part, by grants from the Idaho Commission on the Arts, a State agency, and the National Endowment for the Arts in Washington D.C., a federal agency, and the support of Lewis-Clark State College.

FIRST EDITION

Library of Congress Card Number: 92-70262
ISBN 0-917652-96-7 (paper) / 0-917652-97-5 (cloth)

Published by
Confluence Press
Lewis-Clark State College
Lewiston, Idaho 83501

Distributed to the trade by
National Book Network
4720-A Boston Way
Lanham, Maryland 20706

Sayings For A Dedication Page

T.S. Eliot would sell no poem before its time.

Our literature would be better if
June didn't rhyme with moon.

What the river wrote we can read:
"Build on high ground."

Poetry is all right but I wouldn't want to live there.

To my critics: thanks, anyway.

Contents

My Name is William Tell ► xi
Sniffing the Region ► xiii

1. DOING MY JOB

Today Again ► 3
At Lascaux ► 4
They Carved an Animal ► 5
For Later ► 6
Coyote ► 7
Remembering Mountain Men ► 8
Graydigger's Home ► 9
Out in the Garden ► 10
Inheriting the Earth: Quail ► 11
Roll Call ► 12
Walking at the Zoo ► 13
Priorities at Friday Ranch ► 14
.38 ► 15
Forestry ► 16
Ways to Say Wind ► 17
Snow on the Ground ► 18
Tidepool ► 19
Pacemaker ► 20

2. DREAMS OF CHILDHOOD

One of the Many Dreams of Childhood ► 23
Together Again ► 24
Stereopticon ► 25
Storm ► 26

Old Man by the Road ‣ 27

For a Young Man at an Airport ‣ 28

Tracks in the Sand ‣ 29

Why I Am a Poet ‣ 30

Atwater Kent ‣ 31

A Face ‣ 32

Remembering ‣ 33

Awareness ‣ 34

That Year ‣ 35

In Hurricane Canyon ‣ 36

Scenes of Rain in the Mountains ‣ 37

Waiting by the Sea ‣ 38

A Country Epitaph ‣ 39

3. OUR TOWN OWNED A STORY

The Strange Face on the Sand ‣ 43

A Story for a Winter Night ‣ 44

The Librarian at Fort Yukon ‣ 46

Widow ‣ 47

Vocatus atque Non Vocatus ‣ 48

The Gift ‣ 49

One Man ‣ 50

Today ‣ 51

The Stranger ‣ 52

A History of Our Land ‣ 53

Everything Twice ‣ 54

Storm in the Mountains ‣ 55

Hills ‣ 56

Standing and Knowing ‣ 57

Bedtime Story ‣ 58

At Fort Worden: Calling Names ‣ 59

4. CROSSING THE CAMPUS

Crossing the Campus with a New Generation ▸ 63

Cheat Grass ▸ 64

On the Poly Sci Bulletin Board ▸ 65

Experiments ▸ 66

Dropout ▸ 67

Some Remarks When Richard Hugo Came ▸ 68

At the Thirtieth Reunion ▸ 69

A Wind from a Wing ▸ 70

Someone, Somewhere ▸ 71

A Character ▸ 72

Identity ▸ 73

You, Reader ▸ 74

Index of Titles ▸ 77

My Name Is William Tell

My name is William Tell:
when little oppressions touch me
arrows hidden in my cloak
whisper, "Ready, ready."

Sniffing the Region

Being tagged a regional artist doesn't hurt much. Of course the term may imply accomplishment that is worthy only if assessed locally; but being regional may just mean you use references that seem remote and special because the public is elsewhere and hence limited by immersion in a region distinct from the artist's. So—artists from another region are distinct—"provincial," even—but without adverse reflection on their accomplishment.

And in a sense any artist has to be regional. Doing art takes a kind of sniffing along, being steadfastly available to the signals emerging from encounters with the material of the art—the touches, sounds, balancings, phrasings—and the sequential and accumulating results of such encounters.

To look up from the sniffing, in order to find a critic's approval or a public's taste, is to forsake the trail. And that trail is one-person wide, terribly local and provincial: art is absolutely individual in a non-forensic but utterly unyielding way.

Anyone actually doing art needs to maintain this knack for responding to the immediate, the region; for that's where art is. Its distinction from the academic, the administrative, the mechanical, lies in its leaning away from the past and into the future that is emerging right at the time from the myriadly active, local relations of the artist. Others—administrators, professors, mechanics, or whoever—can of course also be responsive to where they find themselves:—artists have to be. That's the ground for their art, the place where they live.

1. Doing
   My Job

Today Again

Beside my ear the bowstring says,
"I'm just doing my job, goodby,"
and the halves of the bow begin to lament,
"It's yesterday all over again—
Now! Now! Repent! Repent!"

There goes the arrow to break the news:
"This is a world where everything
provides its own best argument,
headlong in being." It all springs alive—
Event. Event. Event. Event.

At Lascaux

It came into my mind that no one had painted
there deep in the ground: if I made a beast,
an arrow into the heart, then aboveground
it would come into my mind again, and
what I hunted, wherever it was, would fall.

Now where I go, daylight or dark,
I hold something still. Before I shoot,
whatever the bow does, and the arrow, and I and
the animal, all come true down deep in the earth:
all that I am comes into my mind.

They Carved an Animal

In a cave somewhere they carved an animal
jumping: that leap stayed. Across the world
in other caves a light gleamed, once.

I stand on a porch under the rain,
and somewhere, you on yours—the rest
of the world leans out, an animal stilled.

There's a leap that lasts in every cave,
but things go on: lights pull into the stars,
a forest springs, I hear the rain.

I touch old boards.

For Later

When I put my foot on this cold road
the moon looked down, a wing came whining
over the field. Nobody warned
or cried out the hurt there is on the way,
when I put my foot on this cold road.

After prayers, after I lost my way,
I wandered here. Is there any place
for starting again, even if years
have passed and I have forgotten,
after prayers, after I lost my way?

In another sky, on another night,
somebody's moon could find what mine
overlooked. All that I missed could be theirs,
and I wish them well, starting out
in another sky, on another night.

Coyote

My left hind-
foot
     steps
in the track of my right
fore-
     foot
and my hind-right
foot
     steps
in the track of my
fore-left
     foot
and so on, for miles—

Me paying no attention, while
my nose rides along letting
the full report, the
whole blast of the countryside
come along toward me
on rollers of scent, and—

I come home with a chicken or
a rabbit and sit up
singing all night with my friends.
It's baroque, my life, and
I tell it on the mountain.

I wouldn't trade it for yours.

Remembering Mountain Men

I put my foot in cold water
and hold it there: early mornings
they had to wade through broken ice
to find the traps in the deep channel
with their hands, drag up the chains and
the drowned beaver. The slow current
of the life below tugs at me all day.
When I dream at night, they save a place for me,
no matter how small, somewhere by the fire.

Graydigger's Home

Paw marks near one burrow show Graydigger
at home, I bend low, from down there swivel
my head, grasstop level—the world
goes on forever, the mountains a bigger
burrow, their snow like last winter. From a room
inside the world even the strongest wind
has a soft sound: a new house will hide
in the grass; footsteps are only the summer people.

The real estate agent is saying, "Utilities . . .
easy payments, a view." I see
my prints in the dirt. Out there
in the wind we talk about credit, security—
there on the bank by Graydigger's home.

Out in the Garden

"Details, details," the mole says;
"few are as worldly as I,
but it pays to have a good coat.
It pays to have a good coat when
you are as worldly as I.

"And I favor my feet a little at the end
of a long day—yes, all four of them.
It pays to favor your feet a little,
at the end of a long day especially,
when you are as worldly as I am."

Inheriting the Earth: Quail

You are supposed to stay still. It won't
always save you, but sometimes it will.
And anyway, little quail, your job is
to go out there and lose, when the time comes.
For awhile you're to call to each other
and scurry for grain. You're to
fly up like a bomb. Learn from their fire
not to make any noise when you die, just
be there—be the evening.
Others have burdens of their own: everyone
does. When you stir at night you can feel
your enemies pray—necessity holding their paws
in its grip, and their own kind of pain in their eyes.

Roll Call

Red Wolf came, and Passenger Pigeon,
the Dodo Bird, all the gone or endangered
came and crowded around in a circle,
the Bison, the Irish Elk, waited
silent, the Great White Bear, fluid and strong,
sliding from the sea, streaming and creeping
in the gathering darkness, nose down,
bowing to earth its tapered head,
where the Black-footed Ferret, paws folded,
stood in the center surveying the multitude
and spoke for us all: "Dearly beloved," it said.

Walking At the Zoo

You move till a step seems
right—move back or on,
depending. I always admire
how the wolf decides where to look.
The last rumble from the lion
ends just before the throat quits
moving. Current in thought, the crane
recalls each leg in sequence, one
bone at a time—it is mathematical.
It saves part of each leg for
next time. But when the wolverine
moves, it summons a leg and
gives it everything.

Priorities at Friday Ranch

1) All that cut juniper west of
   Lava Lake will yield fenceposts
   if you can get there before the crew
   has to clean up for summer.

2) The best tumbleweed you can find
   would look good, hung up for shadows
   about where Dave always put
   his hat by the barn light.

3) If you ever see that gray antelope
   again find out if it has a white
   foot—I think it had a white foot
   on the back left side.

.38

This metal has come to look at
your eye. Look at its eye—that
stare that can't lose.

There's no grin like a gun—
as if only its calm
could soothe your hand.

But metal is cold,
cold. In the night, in the risk,
it's a touch of the dead.

It's a cold world.

Forestry

Old cedars, when the storms come,
hum a fervent anthem
about years, the good life then.

Little trees rustle among
stately trunks that hardly move,
only a slow wind-curtsey.

They hike, the big ones, far
over the pass on good days,
down to a farm's edge at evening.

People walk out and find
the trees discussing religion,
and how to hold your arms when it rains.

Ways to Say Wind

Moves in the woods without
      touching the ground.

Crosses the mountains like a
      scarf between peaks.

From a flat and then kicked-up ocean
      creams along the shore.

Pummels clouds.

Lets a leaf come down in style.

When the sun goes down brings
      the first cold star.

Reminds the valley about snow.

When bushes move talks like
      a rabbit.

Lost all night, calls for
      friends-help-justice.

Remembers the dead.

Snow on the Ground

Whispering our years for the glacier,
carefully they fall, crystal in weightless
flight, confidential as fur, formed without
a breath, looking for their home.

And sometimes a bigger flake forms, a world
in itself, seeking a universe. Once I stuck out
my tongue on the schoolground . . . . I'm five again,
and a bell is calling me in.

Little world, my comfort, teach me my place,
how small a life is amid this long
quiet arrival for everyone waiting
here, where the snow comes.

Tidepool

It is the ocean at home.

It is easy, but it has deep rules.

It is a liquid fact apparently random
　　but riveted together by all the necessities
　　enforced by the universe.

A shadow moves from its place on a rock
　　and hidden dramas adjust their feet
　　for the newest step in the oldest dance.

Something grim tickles its way
　　forward, staring from under mother of pearl.

Minnows play to confuse the sun—
　　they belong to a plot that only
　　the deepest toes in the sand can explain.

Every color has a place and a secret reason.

When the next wave comes, all the others
　　forget what their mission was.

Over in China some child is waiting
　　for all the connected promises in the water
　　that your next step will begin.

Pacemaker

Our slow breath goes out and returns
while the world looms more and more
itself, as dawn at first hasn't arrived,
then has. Our breath makes it happen.
All day it calls forth, minute by minute,
whatever was hiding in the little square
that gradually fills in on the calendar.
At night again we let the world by itself
coast through those hours our breath
quietly monitors, heartbeat, heartbeat.

2. Dreams of Childhood

One of the Many Dreams of Childhood

Floorboards of an old car. Shaking
and rattling and a steady throb under me
as we bump along a country road.
My father talking and driving and Shamosko
beside him, all those knees my backrest
as I crouch under the dashboard, my only
place left, as the family returns late
from a picnic. It is dim down there
and I'm shivering from an icy wind whipping in
from the night. My arm hurts where Mother
jerked me aside when I spilled my chocolate.
The little cave where I huddle is dark
but my own; and I shiver and croon to my hurt arm.
It is only later I learn the words
for my condition: being shunted aside —
neglectful parents; my bruised arm —
battered child; my delicious shivering —
the first stages of *hypothermia*.

Together Again

When I drive, every bridge is
a gift, and the power that swoops
the wires is ready to let go.
The little car radio drinks and drinks
whatever comes out of the sky.

Were our lost ones ever to come
home, and be hale, all four of my
own would come, the center a place
again and the hiss of the river past
a bit of grass the only sound, our whole lives—

And drama enough, this time.

Stereopticon

This can happen. They can bring the leaves back
to the cottonwood trees, those great big rooms
where our street—as long as summer—led
to the river. From a rusty nail in the alley
someone can die, but the street go on again.

Hitler and others, those pipsqueak voices,
can twitter from speakers. I can look back
from hills beyond town, and every person
and all the alleys, and even the buildings
except the church be hidden in leaves.

This can happen, my parents laughing
because they have already won. And I can
study and grow up and look back and call "Wait!"
and run after their old green car
and be lost again.

Storm

On the old highway
thistles are thumbing the wind,
whistling, "Amnesty."

Geese are walking on
their wide pink seismographs and
honking at earthquakes.

They are afraid that
next time they come down earth won't
be there any more.

If I had my life
I would aim it down some old
forest road, again.

Every pond, I
glance aside for a glimpse of
a face in the sky.

Old Man by the Road

You young around me:
I may tend your graves.

You go aggressive ways:
my head patrols the sun.

There is no rock on the mountain
so still as the dreams I dream.

I put you in this one.

For a Young Man at an Airport

It was a still day. Even the engines
were mild. In the waiting room
parents who were as old as I
stood with their child.

He carried a suitcase tied carefully
with string. His good suit fit his
wide shoulders, but I saw him,
as he looked confident and strong:

He could not know, be sure, of anything;
whatever he tried—I knew—might fail.
That careful coat—it told his care
and their long plans, and pride.

I was tired. My health, although all right,
could end. (My suitcase made me hear
my breath.) But when I looked across that
room at you, I saw me years ago,

And I felt sorry for you, my friend.

Tracks in the Sand

For anyone, I am a substitute.
When you were five, kicking the leaves
for a fire, I was you, and the leaves, and the fire.

Or you watch a bomb test—how it mushrooms
over the flat—I am an atom
with the others, and mark you and am your scar.

For anyone else I take the next step
and another, become the road and the sky,
and look back where we were, those tracks in the sand.

For anything lacking—for trees, for rain,
for salvation—I am learning both sides
of the window, and standing between, turning to glass.

Why I Am a Poet

My father's gravestone said, "I knew it was time."
Our house was alive. It moved,
it had a song. The singers back home
all stood in rows along the railroad line.

When the wind came along the track
every neighbor sang. In the last
house I followed the wind—it
left the world and went on.

We knew, the wind and I, that space
ahead of us, the world like an empty room.
I looked back where the sky came down.
Some days no train would come.

Some birds didn't have a song.

Atwater Kent

Late nights the world flooded our dark house
in a dim throbbing from a glowing little box, velvety
sound hovering from horns, or Cab Calloway
far in a night club stretched all the way to Kansas.

Maybe rewarded with popcorn or fudge, maybe
just exhausted by the day, we sprawled on the living room
rug and were carried above our house, out
over town, and spread thin by a violin.

Once from Chicago Enio Bolognini
civilized with his cello a whole
hemisphere, and we were transformed into Italians
or other great people, listening in palaces.

Rich in our darkness, we lay inheriting
rivers of swirling millions, and the promise of never
a war again. It all came from the sky,
Heaven: London, Rome, Copenhagen.

A Face

It's just by chance, who
you are, but given myself
I take care of this being.
Nobody else will remember
its hunger, cold, loneliness:
I will be reminded, and care.

This face, like an old watch,
I carry wherever I go.
Grandmothers, grandfathers, you pictures,
you should forgive my regret:
my wanting another. I carry it
as you did. It belongs
somewhere, and I am taking it there.

On corners I let the wind
have all the world, and I turn
as a ship accepts the waves
but is itself and has a voyage
built into it, stubbornly.

The choice of being who you are
is offered us, or being nothing.
The mask of myself is an old gift
nobody else took. So I brought it here.

Remembering

Long afternoons we swang
through dimes the sun spent
crossing the loft in the barn:
"They couldn't hear a word
if you fell off the world,
there wouldn't be any air,
and they couldn't hear you call—
nothing to touch, no one . . . ."

And we touched the rafters then
where the grain of those old boards
had come out to find the rain,
and the dimes from the sun blessed us
through holes in our overalls
again and again and again.

Awareness

Of a summer day, of what moves
in the trees.

Of your own departing. Of that branch
no one elses notices.

Of time, what it carries, the sideways
drift of it.

Of hiding important things because
they don't belong in the world.

Of now. Of maybe. Of something
different being true.

That Year

The last year I was your friend, they fell
for days "headlong flaming down"—the leaves,
I mean. Aspens heard the news. On the deck
the birdseed sprouted—blue and brown
and rose: two evening grosbeaks came,
trim and ordered, quiet colored,
like Marines. We stood each alone:
the grass had found a tide but we felt none.

When they hurt enough, we let them out—
the words, I mean—and let them trigger
our tongues till they lugered a million times,
like a drum, till the world reversed and leaped,
after its good name. But sunset frisked us for
anything dry or warm, and that year we stood alone:
the grass had found a tide but we felt none.

That year when I was your friend—in words,
I mean—I was afraid. Despite our care
we heard the news. It was more than words.
Persuaded like the grass, we felt the tide
at last: we knew before we were told,
and we shook as the aspens did,
from a storm inside the world.

In Hurricane Canyon

After we talked, after the moon
rose, before we went to bed, we
sat quietly. That was when
we heard the river, big stones
bumping along the bottom from
away up the mountain.

How terribly shredded and lonely
the water went as it cried out and
held splinters of moonlight, and its
life raced powerfully on! That night,
we bowed, shadowed our eyes,
and followed—all the way down—
one, slow, helpless, bumping stone.

Scenes of Rain in the Mountains

First, they show a lake, from right down
by the water looking across, all gray,
dark, with waves and millions of raindrops.
Then they turn. The person to save you
is there, crowded so close you see
only an eye and part of the face,
like an otter, so mild, so benign.
You see how you could have been better if your
days had been different. But it is all right:
You hear the lake and you fall and are saved,
again and again, in the kind eye,
deep and gray, millions of times.

Waiting by the Sea

This tidepool day you inhabit contains more than
you need. It stirs now and then to bring
faint news of old storms deeper than the earth.
From caves around you feelers and claws wave
their greeting, then slowly withdraw
    and wait for tomorrow.

Sunlight is alive when it swims down where you are,
and you stand still, alert to take in the sun.
You become a stone, then a ghost of a stone,
then the gone water's brilliant memory
    of where a stone was.

Making the day expand in your heart and return,
you play a limited part in whatever life is,
practicing for that great gift when enlightenment
comes, that long instant when the tide
    calls your name.

A Country Epitaph

I am the man who plunged
through a river to save his dog;
who failed my parents, though;
who forgot my grief, and sang.

Outside your light I stand.
I appeal through careless words,
I appeal by this casual stone:
Was there more I could have done?

I appeal to human beings:

One day at a time I lived;
I saw more than I told;
I never knew if I claimed
too little or too much. I breathed.

There was more I could have done.

3. Our Town
Owned a Story

The Strange Face on the Sand

Once upon a time our town owned a story—
a beautiful face on the sand my father found
like a statue thrown on an island. "A face
like an angel," he said as he trampled the grass,
"but gone now." "Buried?" we asked. "I suppose."

I touch a branch and listen today—nothing
but truth, steady and low, all that the miles
and years have brought: over the fields
a shadow slides; a mothering wind explores,
too big to be only a story.

But only the shadow of my pen is writing—the pen
carves. Inside each morning, I know where the sky is.
I feel the separate rocks, the touch the hours
make, never losing how the world was then.
"My father found a beautiful face on an island."

Once upon a time our town owned a story.

A Story for a Winter Night

Late one winter night in The North
sleepers awoke in a frozen town:
the whole earth shuddered around their beds
as a chomping monster came over a hill, and down.

And suddenly they remembered—the military post:
a band of men had been told
to build forts up there with a giant machine
that could traverse the cold.

"Ravager," they called it, and they left it running,
its deep engine tame, but the gears tight,
mumbling savagely, its white plume
smoke-ringing deliberately in the moonlight.

Ravager's clang tracks mowed that town.
Its big blade sliced right over a sleeping child.
Then stamping and charging Ravager howled
furiously away into the wild,

Where it still tramps—its great sound
whispering distantly in the northern sky
where now and then a whole mountain avalanches
as it goes inexorably by.

Too big to stop, too strong to wear out, Ravager haunts
those men who let it rear and escape.
They go listening with their children to stand
on the porch or the back step,

As my father took me, the saved child: away off
its blared light flickering its own road, we heard
Ravager feeding on some distant mistake and grunting
hungrily through the night at the adversary world.

The Librarian at Fort Yukon

When parents made moosehide moccasins
our children could walk to school,
but now we need a school bus.

We are careful not to know
where the border is.

My husband came back from the war
and liked the quiet here.

Cold?—yes, but none of us
could ever live anywhere else.

We don't have any crime in the streets—
the bears, you know.

Widow

On the first day when light came through the curtain
a mosquito thought was bothering her—what if
I am important? She wandered the house—the forgiving
table, the surprised-looking bed. Dishes
in the rack needed putting away, and she helped
them. But afterward she regretted—maybe nothing
should move, maybe this day the stillness begins.

She looked out a front window and held every
neighborhood shadow exactly where it was. Then
she carefully X'd out the calendar that had waited
all year for this date. She held out her hand
in a shaft of sun and flexed her fingers, in case
time had passed, in case her body was already gone.

Vocatus atque Non Vocatus

1.

Before life was there a world?
When we take our life away, will fear
be anywhere—the cold? the wind? those noises
darkness tries? We'll take fear
with us. It rides the vast night
carried in our breast. Then, everywhere—
nothing?—the way it was again?

2.

Across a desert, beyond storms
and waiting, air began to make
a wing, first leather stretched on bone
extended outward, shadow-quiet,
then whispering feathers lapped against
each other, and last the air itself,
life taken back, a knife of nothing.

3.

There was a call one night, and a call
back. It made a song. All
the birds waited—the sound they tried for
now over, and the turning of the world
going on in silence. Behind what happens
there is that stillness, the wings that wait,
the things to try, the wondering, the music.

The Gift

Time wants to show you a different country. It's the one
that your life conceals, the one wating outside
when curtains are drawn, the one Grandmother hinted at
in her crochet design, the one almost found
over at the edge of the music, after the sermon.

It's the way life is, and you have it, a few years given.
You get killed now and then, violated
in various ways. (And sometimes it's turn about.)
You get tired of that. Long-suffering, you wait
and pray, and maybe good things come—maybe
the hurt slackens and you hardly feel it any more.
You have a breath without pain. It is called happiness.

It's a balance, the taking and passing along,
the composting of where you've been and how people
and weather treated you. It's a country where
you already are, bringing where you have been.
Time offers this gift in its millions of ways,
turning the world, moving the air, calling,
every morning, "Here, take it, it's yours."

One Man

"Dull Knife," that sound, his name, surrounded
what the wind recovered when it came back
searching over the grass. The bodies had
disappeared, but in his deaf ear the story
found its way, telling itself more slowly than
his life lived: that air talked on after
his tongue was gone, and this world can never
recapture its failure to say that name,
gaining always on history and racing forth
the way it broke through the cavalry that day
he died and escaped and began to wander the earth.

Today

The ordinary miracles begin. Somewhere
a signal arives: "Now," and the rays
come down. A tomorrow has come. Open
your hands, lift them: morning rings
all the doorbells; porches are cells for prayer.
Religion has touched your throat. Not the same now,
you could close your eyes and go on full of light.

And it is already begun, the chord
that will shiver glass, the song full of time
bending above us. Outside, a sign:
a bird intervenes; the wings tell the air,
"Be warm." No one is out there, but a giant
has passed through town, widening streets, touching
the ground, shouldering away the stars.

The Stranger

The place he wanted to tell about
lay beyond, lay far. It had
no name; it hardly differed from this,
but it was apart, and thus deserved
our thought. He spoke on.

There were bushes he wanted us
to see. And the rocks had a certain
subdued gleam when the sun came;
they were not precious, just different,
and other, and odd . . . .

A mountain was there that
you could not see from here.
A stream just smaller than ours bent
and made a park where in winter
deer and elk spelled out their trails.

He spoke on. The world had
such special and lost places in it!
He shook his head when we offered
him a rest. No, no, he would be
getting along. Those bushes—
they had little berries, like salal,
to eat, but sour, but . . . .

After he left I felt insignificant things:
leaf prints on my hands,
at my heels the tug of my shadow,
the hollow away off there, waiting—
towns where we almost lived.

A History of Our Land

In the old times here the hills moved
like big animals. They ate up
villages and climbed on down
into the sea. And the weather then
was always hungry; it fastened
icy teeth deeper every night and returned
for more. In winter it ate up
everything. The stars didn't care
about anybody. They dirlled holes
wherever the clouds opened. Big trees
get together now and whisper their stories
about when bears were the only people.

Everything Twice

One time a green forest one time
around here closed around here
so high a barrier, so high
we couldn't see out at all,
  one time around here so high, at all.

And then came the bear. It came
down the hill, roaring downhill
after us and right here it got us,
coming right through the wall—
  A bear downhill, and got us through the wall.

It happened. Yes, and it happens
you know, its true, you know,
no matter how careful, no matter
how strange, any time at all—
  from the forest, a bear, a disaster, right through the wall.

Storm in the Mountains

Even God can't take the lightning back,
once the old forest wakes in the night and all
the arch of the sky stares aghast at that fall
saved in quiet so long we forgot its attack
that says nothing, nothing till it comes and is over: black
sky again; but cuddled in a snag silent and tall
a fire seed begins a new life so hidden, so small
that no one looks there till another crack
and its eyelids gleam. Oh, the long tumble! The whole
world on its way home somewhere with us helplessly
clinging to keep our place!—clutching our selfish
bodies that finally crash and ignite the soul
to spark, or maybe to spark, maybe to smoulder
while God reconsiders light and dark, over and over
   and over.

Hills

Half of each hill is underground. Moles
know that, and rivers bend more quickly
even just near a hill. Inverted in a lake
a hill signals: "Look, look where I'm pointing."
Usually around a hill are little waves
of ground. When you look at them, you're sorry:
you were going to live there, but somehow
it's wrong—hills take back some things.

Sometimes where hills are a cave interrupts,
and people write messages there. There's a story
about a king who built a hill with a cave,
and the cave was the shape of writing—
long loops and swirls deep there, where
when you walk your feet spell that king's name,
and you keep wondering while you walk,

"Why do I like this king?"

Standing and Knowing

Wherever the mountains put their white gloves on
I know it is still, I know it is still.

Wherever the sea goes back to itself
I know it is still, I know it is still.

Wherever I find the deepest thought
I know it is still, I know it is still.

The land that stretches beyond this hill—
I know it is still.

Bedtime Story

When we animals lived in caves, our mothers
worked hard—help was impossible. They had to carry
whelps outside in their mouths and lick them clean.
And you shopped wherever you could, often by moonlight
or even in the dark, and who knows what
   your whiskers touched
those nights—no roads in the forest of course. And often
it snowed for weeks. The wind howled in the trees,
giants that were dangerous; without warning
they crashed sometimes, and woe to the innocent animal
then. "Too bad," survivors would say and hurry
on by shivering in their fine expensive coats.

Now it is different of course. We have insurance
and some of us keep children for pets. Mothers
are shampooed and pampered; and their whelps
   live like you—
told stories at beditme. But remember—we animals
have relatives everywhere, in those caves
hidden out there in the woods, cozy and dark.
We could move there again—maybe tomorrow.

At Fort Worden: Calling Names

This gun emplacement where we live aims
out there, somewhere—the enemy. We stare
down a barrel where in shadow someone
stands, our president, ready to kill
someone, the enemy. I forget which ones.

These tranquil waters cuddle a shape so hot
its shadow burns your soul, a submarine
that spurns the land. We own it. It prowls
waiting to incinerate what people
we choose. "Our Buchenwald," a fractious bishop
in Seattle calls it—more fire than all the death camps
used. In darkness it glides by.

Our navy wanted to call it *Corpus Christi.*
It slips through Hood Canal.
The Duckabush, the Hama Hama, the Lilliwaup
all wash as well as they can—but there, more fire
than all the death camps patrols the world.
Sleep well, America. The body of Christ glides by,

In our name.

4. Crossing
the Campus

Crossing the Campus
with a New Generation

Practicing how to lose I have perfected
a stillness when I feel the net: a student
mentions a style or a hero, and the world
I had assumed turns over (maybe it is just an
accepting of a fad I abhor—drugs, or terrorism,
or infidelity). I glance away, let the net
hang slack. I escape into something I see,
some steady wall or long vista toward buildings
with slogans at the entrance, *"Fides,"*
"Memoria." I brush against vines when we pass.
Wrong by wrong I am erasing my life in the homeland
behind me. The world has overwhelmed
my kind; the score is thouands to nothing.
Back there when our family fled into
this landscape, we kept saying we would come back—
I hear our old car still trying toward the right
place while a river of shadow floods
our trail through the hills that once moved.

And they will again.

Cheat Grass

If you are reading this, please
turn toward a window. Now think
of a field of cheat grass in a storm,
those little heads doddering and
shining their hint of purple,
but you can't tell why.

If you are still reading this
maybe something about that
grass comes back: it was
a trembling day with strange
noises. Whatever next thing
was coming, nobody knew.

No need to read any more—now
the cheat grass is still running
with the wind, rippling purple
waves. You could see it if
you still lived there. And whatever
the next thing was, it has already happened.

On the Poly Sci Bulletin Board

Wanted: for our study of truth
we need the liars of the world—
Let them come forward.

And we need murderers, plotters,
all the selfish and mean, their
threats, their fiercest raving.

There are not enough people to question, or
to see. A sniffing dog trots through
an honest world: our study is of evasion.

For assignment, consult any teacher
or fill out any blank.
We'll contact you.

Experiments

Part of the cost, we knew, was the pain,
but the budget didn't show that,
and when the animals whined we closed
their door quietly so the accountants
could finish their work and go home.

I wish I didn't know how the universe
runs. I whine now and then when the door
opens or the wind carries what is out there
too near the room where my comfort is.

Dropout

Grundy and Hoagland and all the rest who ganged
our class and wrecked the high school gym for fun—
you thought of them last night, and how they laughed
when they beat up a Mexican.

Later they marched against Hitler youth, but admired
them too—how they were brave and sang: "Why,
you should see how those troopers fought!" And Hoagland
came home to a job with the FBI.

Remember the team?—the celebration in the Lions
Hall?—with Coach Gist there, a real man?—
the speeches?—the jackrabbit chile? You looked through
 the smoke
and the smokey jokes, and vomited.

And never went back again.

Some Remarks
When Richard Hugo Came

Some war, I bomb their towns from five
miles high, the flower of smoke and fire
so far there is no sound. No cry
disturbs the calm through which we fly.

Some day, a quiet day, I watch
a grassy field in wind, the waves
forever bounding past and gone.
Friends call: I cannot look away—

And my life had already happened:
Some saved-up feeling caught, held on,
and shook me. Long-legged grass raced out;
a film inside my head unwound.

The bodies I had killed began to scream.

At the Thirtieth Reunion

That afternoon when it rained
and you shared an umbrella with a freshman
through the college grove—remember?

This is a message propped here
casually, like your gesture that day
for a no one going by alone.

They have had three wars. They have changed
how to live. The grove is gone.
This thanks is for you, so late.

I always intended to find you.

A Wind from a Wing

Something outside my window in the dark
whispers a message. Maybe it is
a prayer sent by one of those friends
forgiving me the years when I sat out their war.
It flared, you know, generating
its own reasons for being, its heroes
anyone killed by an enemy. They looked up
and met fame on a bullet awarded so fast
their souls remained stuck in their bodies,
and then their names, caught on flypaper
citation, couldn't escape. Their families eat that
carrion, and like it. That is their punishment.

In a sky as distant and clear as Pascal's
nightmare, and immediate as our sweat
when God shakes us from sleep, my fate
shudders me awake. Little squeals
of the unborn fly past in the wind. It is midnight
and a motel, and nobody but me remembers
my mother, my father, and that hidden key
they left by our door when I was out late.

Someone, Somewhere

Not you, standing with your host by a window talking,
and not you, poised for light where it falls to admire
what it finds: we are looking for someone different
from any of us, and from those we have always prized.

It isn't "accomplishment," not that. It isn't
how you look, or sound. It may be a helpless
lock on a certain way that no party can change
nor authority dictate outside the room of your mind.

Maybe you choose, and then time begins to deny,
but far somewhere what is yours begins to come,
and nothing—nothing—can stop it between: you have
    turned
a corner and become the self that chose its own prize.

"What must you give," they ask, "to serve the king?"
And you don't have to say, but you know: everything.

A Character

Mobs yell, "Death!" Death separates into
little pieces and falls into their mouths.

People think they can find him by his shadow:
without shadow, he stares into their faces,
his face too obvious for them to see; he
becomes everything, entering it just
ahead of their glance and then waiting there
till they try something else.

Soldiers push him with their bayonets:
his hook follows the back of their skulls.

In the early morning you can hear him
racking up counters, a big, lithe switch-engine
your town has like a pulse in its head.

The young laugh at him. Quietly, he
drinks that kind of laughter.

Out at the cemetery he counts: he will
have a stone under every single drop of rain.

Identity

You are the slow arrival, the coming-to,
the razor slash before your blood believes
(and then it weeps in truth for all the body's theft,
in weltered grief, in its felt need).

You are a premonition lingering on,
the future's parasite down where it lives
in infinite regress of mirrors of the self
past those bone swirls where pieces of childhood drift.

You are the pilgrim watcher clad in black,
a Mennonite along a country road,
through light out there that is extension of your gaze
toward that still hour that any day may hide.

And you are the blundering weaver of self-spun thought
weaving what wants to be woven in the mind,
seeking the praise or blame of some absconded being
whose voice is God's, or only a trick, or wind.

You, Reader

Any night you can awake and line up with the north star.
Any night disguised as a person walking
you can disappear. At the edge of town
darkness comes forward and opens its arms. That star
near the horizon burns its invitation,
"Come on." So many lakes and lost places
wait that you need no plan—there are miles of moonlight
treasuring up waves, and reaches of earth mysterious
as Aladdin's cave. The land rolls out its own
magnificence, and you inherit whatever your eyes
can prove by their glance that they're worthy of.
You listen for music and it comes alive, even
in ordinary sound. The tone of your voice comes back
from the world enriched by all that it passes over.
And this language of ours holds it all.

Now, go back and begin again.

Index of Titles

At Fort Worden:
  Calling Names ▸ 59
At Lascaux ▸ 4
At the Thirtieth Reunion ▸ 69
Atwater Kent ▸ 31
Awareness ▸ 34

Bedtime Story ▸ 58

A Character ▸ 72
Cheat Grass ▸ 64
A Country Epitaph ▸ 39
Coyote ▸ 7
Crossing the Campus
  with a New Generation ▸ 63

Dropout ▸ 67

Everything Twice ▸ 54
Experiments ▸ 66

A Face ▸ 32
For a Young Man at an
  Airport ▸ 28
For Later ▸ 6
Forestry ▸ 16

The Gift ▸ 49
Graydiggers Home ▸ 9

Hills ▸ 56

A History of Our Land ▸ 53

Identity ▸ 73
In Hurricane Canyon ▸ 36
Inheriting the Earth:
  Quail ▸ 11

The Librarian
  at Fort Yukon ▸ 46

My Name Is William Tell ▸ xi

Old Man by the Road ▸ 27
One Man ▸ 50
One of the Many Dreams of
  Childhood ▸ 23
On the PolySci Bulletin
  Board ▸ 65
Out in the Garden ▸ 10

Pacemaker ▸ 20
Priorities at Friday
  Ranch ▸ 14

Remembering ▸ 33
Remembering Mountain
  Men ▸ 8
Roll Call ▸ 12

Scenes of Rain in the
  Mountains ▸ 37

Sniffing the Region ► xiii
Snow on the Ground ► 18
Someone, Somewhere ► 71
Some Remarks When
    Richard Hugo Came ► 68
Standing and Knowing ► 57
Stereopticon ► 25
Storm ► 26
Storm in the Mountains ► 55
A Story for
    a Winter Night ► 44
The Strange Face on the
    Sand ► 43
The Stranger ► 52

That Year ► 35
They Carved an Animal ► 5
.38 ► 15
Tidepool ► 19
Today ► 51
Today Again ► 3
Together Again ► 24
Tracks in the Sand ► 29

Vocatus atque Non Vocatus ► 48

Waiting by the Sea ► 38
Walking at the Zoo ► 13
Ways to Say Wind ► 17
Why I Am a Poet ► 30
Widow ► 47
A Wind from a Wing ► 70

You, Reader ► 74

About the Author

William Stafford was born in Hutchinson, Kansas, in 1914. He has won not only the National Book Award but also the Award in Literature of the American Academy and Institute of Arts and Letters and the Shelley Memorial Award. He has served as Consultant in Poetry for the Library of Congress and on the Literature Commission of the National Council of Teachers of English, and he has lectured widely for the U.S. Information Service in Egypt, India, Pakistan, Iran, Nepal, Bangladesh, Singapore, and Thailand. He lives in Lake Oswego, Oregon.

Cover art by Barbara Stafford-Wilson
Book design and production by Tanya Gonzales
Production assistance by Darinda Schmidt
The type is Baskerville with Goudy display
Printed by Cushing-Malloy on acid-free paper

DATE			